ANIMAL SOS!

SAVE THE TIGER

WINDMILL BOOKS
New York

Published in 2014 by Windmill Books, An Imprint of Rosen Publishing
29 East 21st Street, New York, NY 10010

Produced for Windmill by Calcium Creative Ltd
Editors for Calcium Creative Ltd: Sarah Eason and Rachel Blount
US Editor: Joshua Shadowens
Designer: Emma DeBanks

Photo credits: Cover: Shutterstock: Denise Allison Coyle.
Inside: Dreamstime: Ammit 28, Andy2673 12, Tom Dowd 14,
Erinpackardphotography 15, F9photos 6 bg, Jayanand 21t, Jjspring 26,
Kirsanovv 24, Liumangtiger 9, Lumierephotography 23, Mohdhaka 7,
Neelsky 1, 6, Paulcowan 20–21, Samrat35 13, 22, Scheriton 19, Sean8011 29,
Sekernas 25, T4nkyong 11; Shutterstock: Colette3 4, Defpicture 27, Enciktat
8, David Evison 16, Eric Isselee 5, Joyfull 18, Timothy Craig Lubcke 17,
Tatiana Makotra 12 bg,
Lisette van der Hoorn 10.

Library of Congress Cataloging-in-Publication Data

Royston, Angela, 1945–
Save the tiger / by Angela Royston.
pages cm. — (Animal SOS!)
Includes index.
ISBN 978-1-4777-6029-1 (library) — ISBN 978-1-4777-6030-7 (pbk.) —
ISBN 978-1-4777-6032-1 (6-pack)
1. Tiger—Conservation—Juvenile literature. 2. Endangered species—
Asia—Juvenile literature. I. Title.
QL737.C23R678 2014
599.756—dc23
2013019872

Manufactured in the United States of America

CPSIA Compliance Information: Batch #BW14WM: For Further Information contact Windmill Books, New York, New York at 1-866-478-0556

Contents

Tigers in Danger

Tigers are kings of the jungle! They are incredible hunters and awesome killers, which is why people are so scared of them. However, tigers, not people, are now in danger.

Tigers Are Dying Out

One hundred years ago, 100,000 tigers lived on Earth. Today, only around 3,200 tigers still live in the wild. People are hunting tigers for their fur and bones. Hundreds of tigers are killed every year. People are also cutting down the forests where tigers live to make room for homes and farms.

Unless we do more to save the tiger now, there may be no wild tigers left by 2050.

Gone Forever

Some types of tiger have already died out. Javan, Caspian, and Bali tigers have not been seen for more than 40 years. This book will show you how you can help rescue the tigers still left in the world and make sure they continue to live in the wild.

When tiger mothers are hunted and killed, they leave behind helpless tiger cubs.

Rescue the TIGER!

Environmentalists are working hard to save the remaining wild tigers, and you can help them! Look for photos of these magnificent animals, find out how they live, and what is happening to them. This book is a good place to start! Then tell other people.

Tiger Territory

Tigers are secretive animals. Most of them live alone in places where plants grow close together and there are plenty of animals to hunt. They hide in the **undergrowth** and wait for **prey**.

Where Tigers Live

Tigers come from Asia. At one time they roamed right across Asia, from Turkey in the west to China and Siberia in the east. Today, most wild tigers live in India and Thailand, but others still survive in Siberia and in countries in Southeast Asia.

Thick forest with plenty of bushes is a good place for tigers to hide and to hunt.

Bengal Tigers

More than half of wild tigers are Bengal tigers. They live in different types of forests in India, in the mountains in the north and in rain forests farther south. Tigers need to be close to water, and several live in the swamps among the **mangrove** trees around the mouth of the Ganges river.

Tigers are the only big cats that like to swim. Sumatran tigers have webbed feet that help them to swim faster.

ANIMAL SOS!

Tigers in some countries are more at risk than in others. The number of tigers in Myanmar, Cambodia, Laos, and Vietnam is dropping fast. There are now so few in Myanmar and Laos, it may already be too late to save them.

Tigers' Biggest Enemy

Tigers can easily defend themselves against other animals. Most animals would not dare to attack a tiger, unless the tiger was very young, injured, old, or sick. The tigers' real enemies are people with guns or bulldozers.

Teeth and Claws

Tigers are fierce hunters and fighters. They have sharp claws and teeth, and they run quickly over short distances. Tigers creep up on prey until they are close enough to pounce. Then their deadly teeth rip into the animal's throat or neck.

A tiger has four incredibly long fangs, two on the top jaw and two on the bottom. It uses its fangs to grab its prey and kill it.

No Match

Tigers seldom attack people, but people kill hundreds of tigers. People shoot tigers because they want to sell parts of the animals' bodies. Bulldozers destroy the lands where the tigers live.

South China tigers have lighter colored fur and more black stripes than other types of tiger.

ANIMAL SOS!

The South China tiger is one of the smallest tigers. It used to live in several parts of southern China, but no one has seen it in the wild for more than 25 years. Many scientists think that the South China tiger is now **extinct** in the wild.

Losing Their Homes

Tigers are losing their forests at an alarming rate. Tigers now have only 7 percent of the land they had 100 years ago. What is happening to the tigers' homes?

More People Than Ever

The world's human population is growing fast, particularly in India and Southeast Asia where most tigers live. Extra people need extra farmland and more towns and villages to live in. New roads are built and cut through the forests, breaking up the tigers' **territory**.

The tallest trees in the tigers' rain forests have been growing for more than 100 years. Their wood is good for making furniture, but the trees take a long time to grow back.

Cutting Down the Forests

Logging companies cut down large areas of forest and sell the timber for high prices. Other companies clear land to grow plantations of palm oil, rubber, and other crops, which are sold to people around the world.

Huge plantations of palm oil trees are being planted where tropical forest used to grow. The fruit of the palm is made into oil, which is used in food and as a fuel for vehicles.

Rescue the TIGER!

One of the reasons that the tigers' forests are being cleared on the island of Sumatra, in Indonesia, is to grow coffee beans. Help to save these tigers by telling your family and friends to buy only **sustainable** coffee. This is coffee that has been grown without harm to wildlife or the environment.

Less Food for Tigers

Tigers are not the only animals that lose their homes when forests are cut down. The animals that tigers hunt, such as leopards, deer, and wild pigs, also lose their homes. This makes it even harder for tigers to survive.

Tigers Need Space

Most tigers live alone, but they need enough space to hunt and to meet other tigers in order to produce tiger cubs. Scientists think that female tigers need nearly 8 square miles (20 square km) of territory each, while male tigers need around four times as much.

Tigers crouch low to the ground before they pounce on prey. In cold weather there is less prey for wild tigers and they often stray closer to farms and villages.

Attacking Farm Animals

As their territory is broken into smaller areas, tigers find themselves living closer to farms and villages. Hungry tigers may snatch **domestic animals**, such as goats, dogs, donkeys, and cows. Farmers and villagers then turn on the tigers, killing them to protect their own animals.

Huge machines in an opencast mine break up the ground to reach the coal below the surface. This mine is in West Bengal, which is also home to West Bengal tigers.

ANIMaL SOS!

Mining companies are also breaking into tiger territory. Since 2007, India has doubled the amount of coal it mines. Most of the coal in India, however, lies in central India, where the tigers' largest unbroken territory lies.

Poaching

Poaching is the illegal killing or capture of animals. **Poachers** hunt and kill tigers because they can sell their skins, their bones, and other parts of their body for large sums of money.

Illegal Hunting

Poachers use different ways to kill tigers. They use guns, poison, or even hack them to death with knives. A tiger conservation society in India estimated that almost 900 tigers were killed illegally from 1994 through 2009.

Poachers sometimes camp in the middle of the forest. The poachers set up traps with ropes and nets. They check the traps every day to see what they have caught.

Traditional Medicines

Tiger skins used to be made into rugs or hung on hunters' walls. Today, most tigers are killed to provide ingredients for traditional medicines and tonics. These medicines are very popular throughout China and Southeast Asia, although there is no scientific evidence that they work.

Traditional medicines are sold in markets and stores across China. Each medicine uses different ingredients that are mixed together. Some medicines include parts of a wild animal.

Rescue the TIGER!

Chinese and other traditional medicines are sold in Europe, North America, and other countries around the world. Tell everyone you know to make sure they do not buy traditional medicine that contains tiger ingredients.

Floods and Droughts

Tigers are threatened by rising sea levels and by extreme weather, particularly **droughts**. Both are caused by the temperature at the surface of the Earth becoming warmer.

Losing Land to the Sea

As the sea warms up, it expands, and the sea level rises. Higher seas are eating into low, flat land along the coast. At least 500 Bengal tigers live in the mangrove forests on the Sundarban islands, near the mouth of the Ganges River. Their homes are disappearing below the waves.

Mangrove swamps grow thickly on each side of the rivers in the Sundarbans in India. This is a perfect habitat for tigers, provided the sea does not take over the precious swamps.

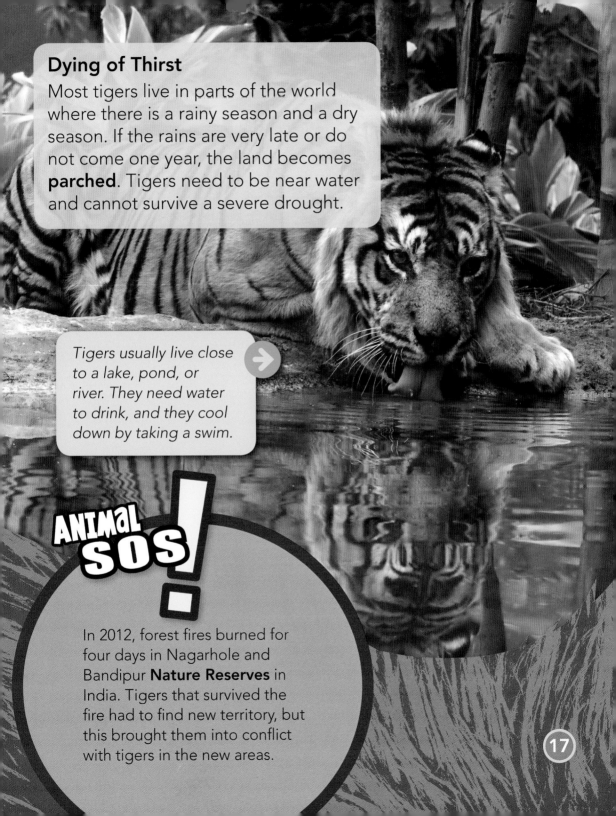

Dying of Thirst

Most tigers live in parts of the world where there is a rainy season and a dry season. If the rains are very late or do not come one year, the land becomes **parched**. Tigers need to be near water and cannot survive a severe drought.

Tigers usually live close to a lake, pond, or river. They need water to drink, and they cool down by taking a swim.

ANIMaL SOS!

In 2012, forest fires burned for four days in Nagarhole and Bandipur **Nature Reserves** in India. Tigers that survived the fire had to find new territory, but this brought them into conflict with tigers in the new areas.

Struggling to Survive

Life is becoming more difficult for tigers. Their territory is being invaded and cleared, and there are fewer wild animals for them to hunt. Roads built through the forest make it easier for poachers to find the tigers there.

No Space to Roam

Not only are tigers losing territory, the land they have left is now scattered and broken up into small patches. This means that groups of tigers are cut off from each other, making it difficult for tigers to meet and produce cubs.

Villages in East Java are being built higher up in the mountains, in the forests where tigers live. Villagers clear some of the land to grow crops.

Tiger Cubs

A tigress has about three cubs at one time. She looks after them in a den for the first two months of their lives, but about half of all wild cubs die before they are two years old. They are killed by male tigers or by **predators**, or they may die of hunger.

For the first few months of their lives, tiger cubs stay in a sheltered den in the forest. As they get bigger, they follow their mother as she hunts prey.

Rescue the TIGER!

Why not hold a tiger party to raise money to save tigers? Draw a tiger on the invitations and ask your friends to dress up as tigers. Give your favorite games a fun tiger slant! "Hide and seek" could become "hide from the tiger!"

19

Tiger Reserves

A nature reserve is an area of land in which wildlife such as tigers is protected. People are not allowed to use the area for farming or mining. The world's first nine tiger reserves were set up in India in 1973.

Setting Up Reserves

Setting up a reserve is not cheap. People who live in the area have to be moved elsewhere. Wardens have to be employed to protect the tigers from poachers. As of 2013, India has 41 tiger reserves, and several more are planned.

Periyar Tiger Reserve is in Kerala, India. The reserve encourages tourists to visit. Boat trips on the lake allow the tourists to see the wildlife from a safe distance.

Helping Others

Tiger reserves benefit all the animals in the protected area, including the animals the tigers prey on. A reserve also helps local people by bringing tourists to the area. In 2012, Bangladesh, Vietnam, Cambodia, Burma, Bhutan, and Nepal asked India to help them set up reserves.

Tigers that live in nature reserves can roam freely in their natural habitat. Some reserves do not allow tourists into the reserve, but other reserves encourage it.

ANIMAL SOS!

India has led the way in setting up tiger reserves, but not all of them have been successful. In 2009, Panna Tiger Reserve had to admit that it had lost all of its tigers to poachers.

21

Protecting Tigers

Protecting tigers is difficult and dangerous! Armed poachers creep into reserves to kill and steal tigers, and companies continue to try to use the land around reserves.

Buffer Zones

Each reserve should be surrounded by a **buffer zone**. This is an area of land that is protected but not as greatly as the reserve itself. Unless the buffer zone is well guarded, companies use it illegally and poachers set traps for tigers that wander into the buffer zone from the reserve.

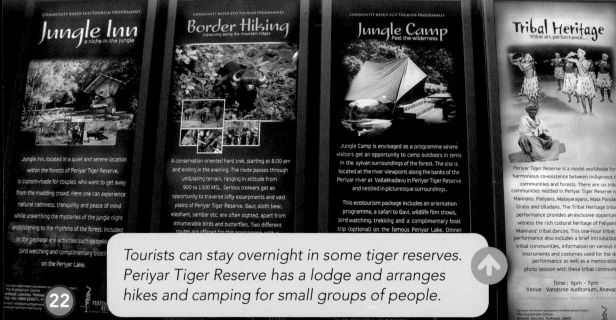

Tourists can stay overnight in some tiger reserves. Periyar Tiger Reserve has a lodge and arranges hikes and camping for small groups of people.

Forest Guards

Local people are trained to work with scientists who care for tigers. They help to keep track of tigers in reserves. Armed guards patrol the reserves and buffer zones, looking for animal traps and poachers.

It is almost impossible to fully protect tigers in a reserve. The tigers can go where they like and it is easy for poachers to hide in the thick undergrowth.

ANIMAL SOS!

Forest guards carry rifles to scare off wild animals and attack poachers. However, in Assam in northeast India, the poachers are often armed with submachine guns. Guards and tigers do not stand a chance against them.

Worldwide Friends

Several organizations have been set up to help tigers and other endangered animals. These organizations raise money and help pay for tiger reserves and other projects. Scientists from the organizations work with governments and experts in the countries where tigers live.

Adopt a Tiger

Conservation societies want more people to help to protect tigers. One way they do this is to encourage members to follow a particular tiger or group of tigers. They give the tigers names and show videos of them on their websites.

Scientists study everything they can about tigers. Examining a tiger's droppings shows what the tiger has been eating.

Tourists

Many tourists want to visit reserves in the hope that they might see a tiger. Scientists disagree about how helpful tourism is to tigers. In India, tourists are forbidden from entering core areas in the nature reserves in case it stops tigers from breeding.

Rescue the Tiger

Join a conservation organization, such as the World Wildlife Fund (WWF) or the Wildlife Conservation Society (WCS). The best way to help tigers is to raise money for one of these organizations. If you adopt a tiger, you can see how your money is being used.

Visiting a tiger reserve can be a fantastic experience, even if you do not see any tigers!

Tigers in Zoos

Zoos keep tigers safe from poachers and they make people aware of these magnificent animals. More than that, scientists in zoos study the tigers to find out how they can best help them in the wild.

Living in Captivity

Tigers need a lot of space and are not happy if kept in cages. The best zoos keep tigers in a large **enclosure** with trees and pools of water, like their natural habitat.

In some private zoos, the zoo keepers train the tigers to jump out of the water to catch colorful pieces of plastic to entertain the tourists.

Tiger Cubs

Tigers breed well in **captivity**. Cubs avoid the dangers that kill wild cubs and so most of them survive. Tiger cubs born in captivity, however, are unlikely to survive in the wild and cannot be used to increase the number of wild tigers.

ANIMAL SOS!

Not all captive tigers are well cared for. In China and Thailand, for example, tiger farms breed tigers in cages. They train the tigers to entertain tourists and sell tiger skins and body parts, particularly the bones, for medicines.

The very best way to see a tiger up close is in a zoo. Thick undergrowth and hideouts in the tigers' enclosure allow them to hide from visitors when they need a rest.

Will Wild Tigers Survive?

The future for tigers is uncertain. Many reserves in India have been successful but others have not, and many tigers in other countries are still losing ground.

Doubling the Number

The WWF wants to double the number of wild tigers by 2022. To do this, more land needs to be protected and forests have to be regrown. One of the best ways of giving tigers more space is to link protected areas with corridors of natural habitat. The tigers can then move easily from place to place.

Male and female tigers usually live separately. They come together when the female is ready to mate and produce cubs.

A Mixed Picture

China, Russia, and other countries want to set up their own tiger reserves, but poachers and tiger farms make it difficult for reserves to succeed. Nature reserves work best when local people are involved in protecting wild tigers, and not in selling their body parts.

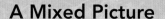

Many adult tigers live alone. Adult tigers stake out a territory, which they then live in and defend from other tigers.

Rescue the TIGER!

Organize a fun run to raise money for tigers. Choose a safe place to run, such as a local park, and ask your friends and family to take part or **sponsor** you.

Glossary

buffer zone (BUH-fur ZOHN) A safe area between two zones, such as a nature reserve and farmland.

captivity (kap-TIH-vih-tee) A place where animals live, such as in a home, a zoo, or an aquarium, instead of living in the wild.

domestic animals (duh-MES-tik A-nuh-mulz) Animals, such as pets and farm animals, which are kept by and looked after by people.

droughts (DROWTS) An unusually long period of time without rain.

enclosure (in-KLOH-zhur) An area, such as a cage or piece of land, that is separated from its surroundings by a barrier.

environmentalists (in-vy-run-MEN-tuh-lusts) People who act to protect the environment.

extinct (ik-STINGKT) No longer existing.

mangrove (MAN-grohv) A type of tree that grows in salty marshes by the sea.

nature reserves (NAY-chur rih-ZURVZ) Areas of land where plants and animals can live safely.

parched (PARCHT) Very dry.

poachers (POH-churz) People who kill wild animals illegally, usually for food or to sell body parts.

predators (PREH-duh-turz) Animals that kill other animals for food.

prey (PRAY) An animal that is hunted by another animal.

sponsor (SPON-sur) Someone who gives money or support to another person to help them achieve a particular goal.

sustainable (suh-STAYN-uh-bul) Grown without damaging wildlife or the environment.

territory (TER-uh-tor-ee) An area of land controlled by a particular animal.

undergrowth (UN-der-grohth) Plants and bushes that grow beneath the trees in a wood or forest.

Further Reading

Ledos, Leah. *Tigers!* The Learning Club. Amazon Digital
    Services, 2012.

Miller, P.K. *Tiger Facts & Pictures*. Amazon Digital Services, 2013.

Milner Halls, Kelly. *Tigers in Trouble!*. Washington, D.C.:
    National Geographic Children's Books, 2012.

Wills, Michael. *Towering Tiger*. Indoor Explorer Book.
    Amazon Digital Services, 2013.

Websites

For web resources related to the subject of this book, go to:
www.windmillbooks.com/weblinks and select this book's title.

Index